Contents

Section One — Sex
Knowing the Score 2
Deciding When to Have Sex 3
What You Want From Sex 4
Myths and Worries About Sex 5
Sex and Relationships 6
Safer Sex 7
Sexually Transmitted Infections 8
Protected Sex 9
Being Attractive 10

Section Two — Having Kids
Pregnancy 11
Your Choices 12
Abortion 13
Bringing Up a Child 14
Choosing to Become Parents 15

Section Three — Prejudice
Racism 16
Disability Prejudice 17
Gender Prejudice 18
Sexuality & Sexual Orientation 19

Section Four — Staying Healthy
Getting Hot and Sweaty 20
Cancer and Meningitis 21
Dealing With Doctors 22
A Bit About First Aid 23

Section Five — Food
Eating 24
Thin, Fat and Diets 25
Eating Healthy Stuff 26
Learn To Cook 27

Section Six — Looking After Yourself
Respecting People 28
Dealing with People 29
Dealing with Trouble 30
Surviving Home Life 31
Keeping Safe 32
Abuse 33
Running Away 34

Section Seven — Mental Health
Coping with Change 35
Feeling Down 36
Stress, Anxiety and Panic Attacks 37
Suicide & Self Harm 38
Eating Disorders 39
Dealing with Mental Health 40

Section Eight — Drugs
Why People Take Drugs 41
Nicotine 42
Alcohol 43
Cannabis 44
Ecstasy 45
Acid, Mushrooms and Speed 46
Heroin, Cocaine and Crack 47
Solvents and Other Nasty Narcotics .. 48

Published by Coordination Group Publications

Contributors:
Taissa Csáky
Charley Darbishire
Andy Park
Alice Shepperson
Jill Webster
With thanks to Glenn Rogers
and Suzie Almond for the proofreading

ISBN: 1 84146 891 6
Groovy website: www.cgpbooks.co.uk
Jolly bits of clipart from CorelDRAW
Printed by Elanders Hindson, Newcastle upon Tyne.
Text, design, layout and original illustrations
© Coordination Group Publications Ltd 2003
All rights reserved.

Section One — Sex

Knowing the Score

Q1 Why is it best to learn about sex before having it? Write down the correct answer.

   a) Because it'll make you more hunky/slinky.

   b) Because people will like you more.

   c) Because your friends will laugh at you if you don't.

   d) Because it'll help you to make choices.

   e) Because it'll be physically painful the first time if you don't.

   f) Because it'll help you understand the consequences.

Q2 List three possible consequences of having sex.

Q3 Write down whether you think the following statements are TRUE or FALSE. Correct any false statements by rewriting them as you think they should be.

   a) It's best to have sex as soon as you can, to get used to it.

   b) Sex is just about physical stuff.

   c) If a bloke has sex with someone who's said, 'No,' he could end up in prison.

   d) You have a right to demand sex if you're in a relationship.

   e) Having sex is a way of proving you're cool.

Q4 How do magazines and TV often portray sex?

Q5 Read the following paragraph about Mark and his girlfriend. What advice would you give to Mark?

   Mark and his girlfriend have been going out for a few weeks.

   They haven't had sex because his girlfriend says she doesn't feel ready yet.

   Most of Mark's friends say they are already having sex with their girlfriends, and they laugh at Mark because he's not 'doing it'.

   They keep telling him he should force his girlfriend to have sex whether she wants to or not.

Deciding When to Have Sex

Q1 When should you start having sex? Choose the correct answer from below and write its letter down.

> a) When a big red light goes on above your head.
> b) When your friends tell you it's OK.
> c) On your 16th birthday.
> d) When you feel ready for it.
> e) When you start going steady with your partner.
> f) After you've discussed it with your parents.

Q2 What's the most sensible thing to do if you're not sure whether you're ready for sex?

Q3 Give one good reason why waiting until you're ready for sex is worth it.

Q4 Copy and complete the paragraph, using the right word(s) from the list below:

> 16   prison   school   sentence   criminal record
>
> 18   law   police   public   more serious

> You could end up with a .... if you have sex with someone under 16. Having sex with a girl under 13 is .... and could land you in .... Gay men who have sex in .... can be prosecuted if they are found out. A teacher who has a sexual relationship with a pupil under .... can get into serious trouble.

Q5 What advice would you give to Sharmila in the situation below?

Sharmila doesn't have a boyfriend and has never had sex.

She feels left out because all her friends are dating and having sex with their boyfriends.

A boy she meets at a party asks her to have sex with him. Although she doesn't fancy him, she thinks she should do it, just to keep up with her friends.

Do you think Sharmila should have sex with the boy? Give reasons why/why not.

Section One — Sex

What You Want from Sex

Q1   Girls just want relationships, blokes just want sex. True or false?

> All girls just like toast, while blokes <u>only</u> like cereal. True or false? Or a daft question?

Q2   Sometimes, Alex would rather have a cuddle with his girlfriend than have sex with her. Is Alex:

   a)   normal?

   b)   gay?

   c)   weird?

   d)   a total loser?

> Only one of these is right.

Q3   If you have sex with someone, will it make them love you?

Q4   Which of the following are bad reasons for having sex?

a need to feel loved	to keep a boyfriend or girlfriend	because you owe someone money
because all your mates say they're doing it	to win a bet	to prove you're not gay

Q5   Does having sex make you more attractive or popular?

 Q6   How should Cheryl react in the situation below?

Tom has spent a small fortune on Cheryl on their first date.

He bought all her food and wouldn't hear of it when she tried to buy her own drink in a bar.

Should Cheryl agree to have sex with Tom because he's spent so much money on her?

> No?! But those potatoes and cartons of prune juice cost me a small fortune?!

Section One — Sex

Myths and Worries About Sex

Q1 If a boy has one testicle hanging lower than the other, it's a sign that:

a) he's not ready to have sex

b) he's perfectly normal

c) he should see a doctor immediately

d) he's not a virgin

Q2 What's the name of the flap of skin that gets broken when a girl has sex for the first time?

a) prostate   b) hymen   c) gland   d) vagina

Q3 Why might having sex for the first time be a bit of a disappointment?

Q4 Copy and complete the following sentence using a word or phrase from the box:

The only 100% effective way to avoid pregnancy is ....

| to not have sexual intercourse at all | to do it standing up |
| to keep your shoes on | to keep one foot on the floor |

Q5 Write down whether you think the following statements are true or false:

a) You have to do oral sex even if the idea grosses you out.

b) Sperm can't reach the egg if you do it standing up.

c) It's harder for a girl to get pregnant if it's her first time.

d) Pulling out before the boy comes is a good contraceptive.

e) You can't get pregnant if you do it while you're on your period.

f) Loads of people with the HIV virus caught it in their teens.

g) You can only catch chlamydia if you're over 20 years old.

 Q6 What would you say in the following situation? Is she right?

A girl at school tells you that you can't get pregnant if you have a shower straight after sex. She says she's done it lots of times without using a contraceptive and has never got pregnant.

Section One — Sex

Sex and Relationships

Q1 Having sex with someone is proof that you love them. True or false?

Q2 When's the right time to start having sex with someone? Choose from the answers below.

    on your first date   *when you need to feel loved*

    after you've told them you love them   *when you're bored*

    when you both feel ready   *when you want an orgasm*

Q3 What should you do (or not do) if you're too shy to talk about sex with your boyfriend or girlfriend?

Q4 Copy and complete the following paragraph using words from the box:

> intimate   a relationship   selfish   trust
> different   contraception   reality

If you're in ...., then sex is likely to be on the agenda at some point. Before you have sex, it's important that you and your partner .... each other. Talking about .... before having sex is a good plan. Most people feel .... after sex.

Q5 Sarah and Jim have decided they are both ready to have sex. Suggest the kind of things they might want to discuss before getting naked together.

You'll need to think about practical things, for sure.

But you should also think about emotional stuff too.

Don't believe everything you hear — get your facts right...

"Sex, sex, sex — that's all you see on telly these days..." Hmmm, maybe, but that doesn't mean you can believe all you see and hear. The more you know about sex (really know, that is — as opposed to having heard from a mate who saw something on telly once), the more likely you are to make sensible decisions.

Section One — Sex

Safer Sex

Q1 Complete the following sentence by choosing the best word from the box:

Safer sex is ....

> boring   unnecessary   vital
> optional   stupid

Q2 What should you use to avoid getting diseases from oral sex?

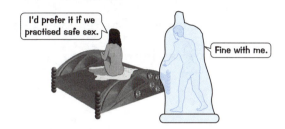

Q3 List two things that could happen if you have sex without a condom.

Q4 What should you always do if you decide to have anal sex?

Q5 While masturbation is natural, there are times and places that it is inappropriate. Which two of the following suggestions should you follow to avoid inappropriate behaviour?

> a) don't do it in public
> b) use contraception
> c) don't fall asleep afterwards
> d) don't do it in front of anyone who hasn't said they want to watch
> e) wear a full set of body armour
> f) don't use baby oil

Q6 Andrew and Katy don't feel ready to have full penetrative sex yet, but they would like to get sexy with each other.

What kind of things can they do to explore sex safely?

Section One — Sex

Sexually Transmitted Infections

Q1 How can you catch an STI? Write down the correct letter.

> a) from toilet seats
> b) by kissing
> c) from having unprotected sex
> d) from mosquitoes
> e) from the swimming baths
> f) by drinking from the same cup

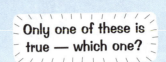
Only one of these is true — which one?

Q2 List four telltale signs that could mean you have an STI.

Q3 What's the most common STI for 16-19 year olds?
Why is it important to get it checked out if you think you might have it?

Q4 Copy and complete the following sentences:

> a) Your doctor isn't allowed to talk to your parents about you unless…
> b) Gonorrhoea can be treated by…
> c) Crabs make you itch because….
> d) Sharing needles for injection is dangerous because…
> e) Even catching the flu can be dangerous if you have AIDS because…
> f) Thrush doesn't always come from sex. You can also get it if…

Q5 Read about Sharon and Stephen. Then decide what you think each of them should do in the following situation:

Stephen had unprotected sex several times with different girls before he met his steady girlfriend Sharon.

Stephen and Sharon have been together for two months.

Sharon is on the pill, and Stephen doesn't wear a condom when they have sex.

Last week, Sharon noticed a small sore on her vagina.

Section One — Sex

Protected Sex

Q1 What's the difference between contraception and safe sex?

Q2 Which one of the things listed below protects you from both pregnancy and STIs?

> taking the pill   taking the morning-after pill
>
> having sex standing up   using a coil   having a hot bath after sex
>
> wearing a condom / femidom   using baby oil or vaseline

Q3 The box below shows a load of statements about condoms. Decide whether each one is true or false. Rewrite the ones that are false so that they are correct.

Using a condom is 99% effective if...

1. ...you remove it immediately after sex.
2. ...you use the same condom more than once.
3. ...you stop halfway through sex to put one on.
4. ...your nail snags the condom as you're putting it on.

Q4 Use the correct words from the list below to complete the following paragraph:

> combined   hormones   diaphragm   coil
> morning-after   temperature   fertilisation

There are two types of contraceptive pill — the .... pill and the progesterone-only pill. The pill works by changing the .... in a woman's body. Other forms of contraception for women include the ...., which is a little rubber bowl that fits over the cervix, and the .... , a T-shaped plastic and wire device that fits inside the womb. The .... pill isn't a contraceptive, it's an emergency measure that you can take up to 72 hours after unprotected sex.

Q5 Susan and Mark were using a condom but it ripped while they were having sex. This happened 24 hours ago.

What do you think Susan and Mark should do in this situation?

You really do want to know about this stuff...

If you're gonna do it, do it safely. And doing it safely doesn't just mean not getting pregnant — it means not ending up with icky stuff dripping out of places that you really don't want it dripping from. Okay.

Section One — Sex

Being Attractive

Q1   What's the difference between being 'attractive' and being 'good-looking'?

Q2   Which of these is important for pretty much everyone when it comes to looking attractive?

- a)   wearing designer clothes
- b)   making the most of what they've already got
- c)   having a hunky/slinky body
- d)   looking gormless
- e)   being famous
- f)   having lots of admirers

There's only one right answer in here. Write down the correct letter.

Q3   Are good looks a passport to happiness? Give reasons for your answer.

Good looks haven't always brought me happiness.

Q4   Write down whether the following statements are true or false:

- a)   Attractiveness has nothing to do with the way you behave.
- b)   Personality is often the most important part of falling for somebody.
- c)   Outgoing people are more attractive than quiet types.
- d)   Being really cocky and arrogant is usually very attractive.
- e)   The best way to be attractive is to be yourself.

Q5   Stephen doesn't think he'll ever pull, because he's 6 feet tall and skinny. He walks around with a stoop to try and disguise his height, and he blushes whenever a girl talks to him.

What advice would you give Stephen if he asked you how he can make himself more attractive?

Section One — Sex

Section Two — Having Kids

Pregnancy

Q1 How many teenage pregnancies are there in Britain every year?

    a) about 10,000

    b) about 50,000

    c) about 90,000

Q2 If a sexually active girl misses her period, what should she do?

Q3 Name two places other than a chemist where you can get a pregnancy tester kit.

Q4 Copy and complete the following sentence, using the best phrase from the box:

> change colour   give off a weird smell   vibrate
>
> make a noise like a quacking duck   taste of raw potato

Pregnancy tester kits work by checking for chemicals in your pee.

If you are pregnant they ………………………… .

Q5 What should you do if you have unprotected sex or your condom splits?

    a) wait to see if the woman misses her period

    b) hope for the best

    c) visit your doctor or clinic straight away for the morning-after pill

    d) forget about it

    e) get a pregnancy tester kit

Q6 Pam's period is 4 days late and she is worried that she may be pregnant. She finally plucks up the courage to tell her boyfriend Charlie.

How do you think Charlie should respond?

Your Choices

Q1 In what ways can being pregnant change a woman's lifestyle? Choose from the box below:

> She has to give up drinking and smoking.
>
> She may puke a lot.
>
> She can't go out much.
>
> She may get upset more easily.
>
> She has to put up with getting bigger and bigger over the next 9 months.

This means the actual 'being pregnant' part, not the bit afterwards when the kiddy's been born — the changes then are bigger still.

Q2 The baby's dad only has parental rights in law if:

   a) ...he decides he wants parental rights.

   b) ...he's married to the baby's mum.

   c) ...he's over 16.

   d) ...the mother has agreed to give him parental rights.

   e) ...he can prove he can support a family.

   f) ...he's got a court order giving him parental rights.

Three of these are right. Write down which ones.

Q3 What choices does a girl have if she's pregnant?

Q4 Describe what happens if a girl decides to give her baby up for adoption.

Q5 Who should a girl definitely tell if she decides to have her baby? Why?

 Q6 Marion has just found out that she's pregnant. She hasn't decided what to do about the baby yet.

   What kind of things will she want to consider?

   Who might she want to tell to help her reach her decision?

Section Two — Having Kids

Abortion

Q1 How long can you legally wait before having an abortion?

   a) 6 weeks

   b) 12 weeks

   c) 24 weeks

   d) 1 year

Q2 What do two doctors need to agree before a woman can have an abortion?

Q3 Copy and complete the following paragraph by filling in the gaps with the right number from below:

   24   13   2   9   12

   Most abortions are carried out within .... weeks of conception. A woman

   needs to get the agreement of .... doctors before she can have an abortion.

   If the foetus is less than .... weeks old, the woman is given an 'abortion pill'.

   After .... weeks, she will need to have an anaesthetic to have the abortion.

   Abortions are only allowed after .... weeks if the pregnancy would endanger

   the mother's life or if there is something wrong with the foetus.

Q4 Can a man legally stop his wife or girlfriend from having an abortion?

Q5 If you have an abortion you can't have children later in life. True or false?

Q6 Name two private organisations where you can pay for contraception and abortion services.

 Q7 Amanda is 14 weeks pregnant. She has been worrying what to do for ages, and has now decided to have an abortion.

   Explain the type of abortion she is likely to have, and how she might feel afterwards.

Section Two — Having Kids

Bringing Up a Child

Q1 Being a parent means you're responsible for the child until:

...it can walk.   ...it can talk.   ...it's 18 years old.

...it leaves home.   ...it goes to school.

Q2 Decide whether you think the following statements are true or false:
   a) Having a baby doesn't change your life that much.
   b) You have a legal right to live with your parents when you've had a baby.
   c) The money you spent on clothes and going out gets spent on the baby.
   d) Babies never cry during the night.
   e) It's OK to go out for an evening and leave the baby on its own.
   f) It's OK to go back to your education once the baby starts to grow up.

Q3 Why is it more difficult for people to keep in touch with their friends after they've had a baby?

Q4 Copy and complete the sentence using the right phrase from below:

   a parent   *breast-feeding*   *living at home*   *a werewolf*   *on a night out*

   Drinking and smoking are off-limits when you're ....

DISCUSSION QUESTION

Q5 Anthony and Tess are both 15. They have just had a kid, Ant. They are all going to live with Tess's parents till they get sorted financially.

   What kind of lifestyle changes are they going to have to get used to?

   Think about as many aspects of their lives as you can. This will include things like: education, socialising, hobbies, relationships, finances, etc.

Section Two — Having Kids

Choosing to Become Parents

Q1 Which of the following are reasons why some people choose to wait before they have kids?

> They want to get married first.   They haven't enough money yet.
>
> They haven't had the urge to have kids just yet.

Q2 Why can it be a mistake to have a child just because you want someone to love you? What could be the consequences?

Q3 Copy and complete the paragraph by filling in the gaps with the right words from below:

>   borrow   relationship   tax   adopt   fact
>
>   fertility   law   stable   family   money   legal

> Wanting kids is a .... of life for many people. Some people decide to wait till they've got enough .... before starting a family. People who have problems conceiving can have .... treatment or they can .... a child. It's easier to raise a child in a .... relationship because you can work together as a team. Marriage means that two parents are bound together by .... There are also .... benefits for married couples with children.

Q4 Getting married just because you're expecting a baby is a good idea. True or false?

Q5 Emma has been going out with her boyfriend Dave for 10 months. They used to get along great, but recently they seem to have done nothing but argue. Emma thinks that if she gets pregnant, it'll make Dave love her more and they won't argue any more.

Do you think it's a good idea for Emma to try to get pregnant now?

Why/why not?

Baby... maybe... — but maybe not just yet...

Deciding to have kids is a heck of a big decision — so if you (or your girlfriend) get pregnant, there's a shedload of things to think about. But in that situation, the more you know, the better off you are.

Section Two — Having Kids

Section Three — Prejudice

Racism

Q1 Write down as many ethnic backgrounds as you can think of for people living in the UK today.

Q2 Over the years, people have come to live in the UK for lots of different reasons. Write out all the possible reasons from the box below:

> To get away from a war
> For the mild weather
> As part of a military invasion
> To avoid being arrested for a crime
> Because they think it's pretty here
>
> To get away from a repressive government
> To get away from religious persecution
> To escape from racist attitudes
> To get a job
> To learn English

Q3 All of these ways of behaving could be called racist. Which of them is illegal?

a) Setting fire to a shop because the owner is Pakistani.

b) Not bothering to say hello to the new Kurdish boy in your class.

c) Shouting abuse at somebody because he's Muslim.

d) Picking a fight with somebody because he's German.

e) Refusing to give a nurse a job because she's Kenyan, even though she's got all the right qualifications and experience and speaks excellent English.

DISCUSSION QUESTION Q4 Mildred's gran says all Palestinians are terrorists.

Work out what to say in a letter to Mildred's gran, explaining why what she says isn't true.

DISCUSSION QUESTION Q5 Read through the situation then answer the questions:

> Darren and Sagal are both in your class. Darren was born and brought up in your town. Sagal was born in Somalia. Darren keeps making comments about Sagal's appearance and name, and telling her she "doesn't belong" here. Sagal is getting upset and stressed by Darren's behaviour.

What do you think Sagal should do about the abuse from Darren?

What would you do in this situation? What would you say to Darren and Sagal?

Disability Prejudice

Q1 In each pair below, there's one way of talking about disability that's offensive and one that's not. For each pair, say which is the offensive term and explain why the other one's better:

   a) handicapped person / disabled person

   b) spastic / has cerebral palsy

   c) wheelchair-user / wheelchair-bound

   d) disabled people / the disabled

Q2 Explain how Robin could have handled each of these situations better:

   a) Robin's football team is one man down for the all-important Yeovil Local Yokel League match. Bryan says his cousin Boris is staying for the weekend and he could play in the match. Robin says there's no way Boris can play — he's deaf.

   b) Robin sees a really pretty girl on the bus. He's about to go and talk to her when he sees her guide dog and realises she's blind. He feels all awkward and embarrassed and decides not to talk to her after all.

   c) A woman and a man come into the café where Robin works on Saturdays. The man, who's in a wheelchair, asks for a coffee. Robin says to the woman, "White or black?"

   d) The man from the café can't hold his head straight so he drinks his coffee with a straw. Instead of clearing up the other tables, Robin leans on the counter staring.

DISCUSSION QUESTION Q3 Many deaf people don't think of themselves as disabled.

Do you agree?

Make a list of bullet points explaining what you think "being disabled" means.

DISCUSSION QUESTION Q4 If there are disabled people at your school or you are disabled:

Make a list of the ways life at your school is different for the disabled and non-disabled people.

OR If there are no disabled people at your school:

Imagine that somebody who is paralysed and uses a wheelchair is joining your class.

How will life at school be different for them? How will the school routine have to change?

Section Three — Prejudice

Gender Prejudice

Q1 Read the definition of sex discrimination, then say whether you think each situation below is an example of sex discrimination. Answer "yes", "no" or "depends", and explain why.

> "Sex discrimination is treating people unfairly because of their gender."

a) Mark and Maeve are both trained pilots. They have the same qualifications and experience. Mark applies for five jobs, gets five interviews, and gets a job. Maeve applies for five jobs and doesn't get any interviews.

b) For their eighth birthday the twins Fatima and Yasmin ask for remote-controlled jeeps. Their parents get them a doll's house.

c) Martin phones Mike, Lenny and Stu to ask whether they want to play football. He doesn't ask Wendy.

Q2 Say whether each of these statements is true or false:

a) Women can join the Army, Navy and Air Force, but they're not allowed to fight on the front line.

b) Men get custody of the kids more often than women if they get divorced.

c) In the UK, men and women always get the same pay for the same work.

d) A man is entitled to time off work when his baby is born. Employers don't have to pay him while he's away, though.

e) There are equal numbers of men and women in top management jobs in the UK.

f) Men get less support than women if they get abused by their partners.

DISCUSSION QUESTION Q3 Do you agree with this statement?

> "There are some jobs which are better suited to men, e.g. being a front-line soldier, and some which are better suited to women, e.g. teaching a reception class."

DISCUSSION QUESTION Q4 Have you ever been treated in a way you didn't like and thought it was because of your gender?

Think about little niggly things, e.g. people talking to you in a way you found a bit patronising, as well as bigger stuff, e.g. not being allowed to join the rugby/ synchronised swimming team.

Lads, this one's for you too. Gender prejudice rubs both ways.

Sexuality and Sexual Orientation

Q1 Copy the sentences below and fill in the gaps with words from the box. You'll have to use the words more than once.

opposite   same

a) Gay people are attracted to people of the .... sex.

b) Straight people are attracted to people of the .... sex.

c) People who are bisexual are attracted to people of the .... sex and people of the .... sex.

Q2 True or false?

a) Most paedophiles are homosexual.

b) Most gay men are also attracted to young boys.

c) Sex between gay men is illegal.

d) Physically attacking someone for being gay is illegal.

e) Refusing to give somebody a job because they're gay is fine, especially if the job involves contact with young children.

Q3 Why is the stereotypical image of gay men as camp and lesbians as butch inaccurate?

DISCUSSION QUESTION Q4 Do you agree with any of these statements? Explain why.

"I don't care what they do, so long as I don't have to see it, hear it or talk about it."

"Live and let live."

"Homosexuality is probably genetic. If it is, then being gay is as 'natural' as being straight."

"Homosexuality is a terrible sin. It says so in the Bible."

DISCUSSION QUESTION Q5 Why do you think some people have such strong opinions about homosexuality?

Try and think of as many reasons as you can.

Everyone's different, everyone's the same...
Some people still get really upset by the idea of homosexuality. Even if you personally disagree with it, there's no excuse for laying into other people for being gay. End of story. Finito. Basta. The End.

Section Three — Prejudice

Section Four — Staying Healthy

Getting Hot and Sweaty

Q1 Write true or false for each of these sentences:

a) Only sporty people should do exercise.

b) It's not worth doing exercise unless you keep going until you puke or pass out.

c) You can fit more exercise into your routine by doing things like walking to the shops instead of taking the bus.

d) Yoga, dance and self-defence are too easy — they don't count as proper exercise.

e) It is a good idea to warm up with some stretches before you start exercising.

Q2 Copy and complete this paragraph, filling in the gaps with words from below:

> Exercise makes you feel more cheerful by releasing chemicals called .... in your brain. Regular exercise can help you avoid .... and .... As you exercise more you'll notice that your .... get firmer and you start standing up straighter. The more you exercise, the more .... you burn, so you'll find if you exercise regularly you start ...., or you can eat .... without ....

    more   depression   muscles   putting on weight
    energy   endorphins   losing weight   stress

Q3 What can you say to these people to persuade them that exercise is a good idea?

a) "I'm in a really bad mood. I just don't feel like playing football."

b) "I hate doing exercise — it's so embarrassing wearing lycra in front of all those super-fit people at the gym."

c) "I just feel knackered after I've been for a run. How can you say exercise gives you energy?"

DISCUSSION QUESTION Q4 The last exercise Karina did was playing kiss chase at primary school. But she's decided to get off the sofa and get fit.

Write an exercise plan for Karina to follow, building up to doing at least half an hour of energetic exercise three times a week.

DISCUSSION QUESTION Q5 Think about how much exercise you do in an average week.

Write down all the exercise you do in a week and how long you spend doing it.

Compare the amount of exercise you do with the rest of your group. Suggest ways for each other of fitting more exercise into your week.

Write yourself a new exercise plan based on the suggestions.

Cancer and Meningitis

Q1 List three ways meningitis can spread.

Q2 You need to watch out for the symptoms of meningitis. Find them in the box below.

> high temperature and fever   really bad headache   vomiting
>
> rash (and the spots don't fade when you press them with a glass)
>
> blue tongue   can't stand bright lights   stiff neck
>
> big Adam's apple   swollen stomach   diarrhoea

Q3 Copy and complete the sentences below about glandular fever. Use the words around the kissing on the right.

> Glandular fever isn't really .... — it just makes you .... for about a month. You get it from coughing / .... / snogging — it used to be called the '.................. disease'. If you've got a sore throat, ... and flu symptoms, then go to the doctor.

swollen glands, knackered, sneezing, serious, kissing

Q4 *You should check your breasts (if you're a lass) or testicles (if you're a lad) every couple of weeks for signs of cancer.*

What are the signs of cancer that you should be looking for? What should you do if you find anything?

DISCUSSION QUESTION

Q5 It's a hot and sunny day in July. Jessica has been sunbathing without protection for five hours.

In what ways has she been stupid? Think about the short and long term risks.

DISCUSSION QUESTION

Q6 *Jason isn't feeling well and there was recently a case of meningitis at his school.*

Write a series of questions to ask Jason, to see whether he's got meningitis.

Remember — the big difference between meningitis and other infections is that it needs to be dealt with right away or it could be fatal.

Section Four — Staying Healthy

Dealing with Doctors

Q1 Which of these describe your doctor's job? Write out the correct answers.

- The doctor helps the patient decide on the best treatment.
- The doctor answers all the patient's questions so they can understand what's happening to them.
- The doctor is very important and shouldn't be bothered with stupid questions.
- The doctor should explain everything to the patient very quickly so he's not late for his game of golf.
- The doctor decides what happens to the patient.
- The doctor should always explain what's going on clearly, in language the patient understands.

Q2 Why don't you need to visit the doctor or get antibiotics if you've got an ordinary cold?

Q3 If you're under 16, where can you go for confidential advice on...

a) sexually transmitted infections?

b) contraception?

c) pregnancy?

Q4 You don't always need to go to the doctor for minor illnesses. Write down three other places you can get medical advice without making an appointment at the surgery.

Q5 Write out these sentences with the right words from each pair:

a) When you want to change your doctor you **don't have to / have to** explain why.

b) You **can / can't** change doctors if you'd rather have a doctor of the opposite sex.

c) You **can / can't** change doctors if you don't agree with the treatment your doctor suggests.

DISCUSSION QUESTION Q6 Decide whether each of these people should change their doctor...

Madge's doctor has bad breath and dandruff and there's a really fit young doctor who's just joined the surgery.

Arun's doctor always keeps him waiting at least half an hour for appointments then rushes through Arun's appointment because he's running late.

Chloe went to see her doctor about very painful periods. He told her the only practical option was a hysterectomy. Chloe doesn't agree.

Section Four — Staying Healthy

A Bit About First Aid

Q1   What's the best way to learn about first aid?

a) looking at websites;

b) reading lots of books about it;

c) going on a course;

d) watching ER?

Q2   You and your mate find a man lying in the middle of the road unconscious. There's nobody else about. Put these steps in order to say what you should do to help him.

> Give first aid IF you know what you're doing.
>
> One person gets an ambulance.
>
> One person stays and works out what's happened.

Q3   What should you do in each of these situations?

a)

b)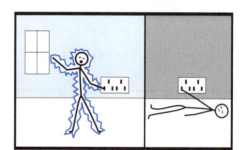

c)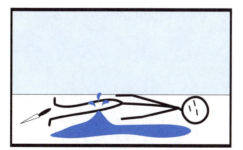

d)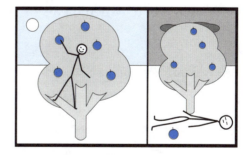

Q4 (DISCUSSION QUESTION)   Have you or anyone in your group ever had to deal with a first-aid situation?

Make notes of what happened in each situation. Decide as a group whether there were better ways of dealing with the situation.

Make an action plan for the best way of handling similar situations in future.

Stay calm — there's no cure for losing your head...

This is serious stuff — literally life or death. Don't panic about it, just get yourself booked on a first-aid course. Or, for light relief, watch a bit of ER and daydream about Dr Kovacs. Then book that course.

Section Four — Staying Healthy

Section Five — Food

Eating

Q1 High-society nutritionist Cornelia Compton-Corset has written a bestseller called *Fabulous Eating* — it's a load of tosh. Rewrite Cornelia's Food Rules, adding a dash of common sense:

> 1. Mind over matter at all times. Never eat when you are hungry.
>
> 2. The one sure cure for feeling bored or lonely is a delicious cream bun or three.
>
> 3. Skip breakfast and lunch whenever you can.
>
> 4. One should chew one's food as little as possible.
>
> 5. If you are having seconds, have them straight away, before you feel too full for more.

Q2 Choose the most sensible advice from each pair:

a) • Teenagers need to eat about half the amount that adults eat.
   • Teenagers need to eat more than adults because they need more energy.

b) • If you want to make sure your breakfast really fills you up, eat lots of cereal or bread.
   • If you want to make sure your breakfast really fills you up, have lots of chocolate.

c) • Never, ever, ever eat between meals.
   • It's fine to eat between meals — but only if you're actually hungry.

DISCUSSION QUESTION

Q3 Look at these food diaries:

Daphne
Breakfast: Apple on the school bus.

Lunch: 2 cigarettes and a packet of crisps

After school: chips

Tea: microwave pizza.

Doris
Breakfast: tea, toast and Marmite

Lunch: ham & tomato sandwich, apple, yoghurt

After school: Marmite sandwich. Three slices of cake.

Tea: chicken, mash, salad

Who do you think is eating better? Write down all the reasons why.

Write an action plan for the person who's not eating so well, suggesting some ways she could eat better.

Thin, Fat and Diets

Q1 For each of these sentences say whether it's true or false:

a) Diets designed for adults are fine for teenagers too.

b) The thinner you are, the healthier you are.

c) If you're too thin you pick up bugs more easily.

d) It's healthier to be too thin than too fat.

e) Attractive people are always thin.

f) Thin people are always attractive.

g) People are naturally different shapes and sizes.

Beware: people who are too thin can pick up bugs easily

Q2 Write out the words below under two headings — "Good Diet Advice" and "Bad Diet Advice".

| Don't totally cut out any type of food. | Skip meals. If you feel hungry have a cigarette. | Cut down a bit on everything you eat. | Don't eat any fish. |

| Take laxatives. They don't give your body time to digest the food. | Eat more fruit, veg, bread, rice and pasta and less fatty, fried foods. | If in doubt, check with the doctor whether you really are overweight before you start dieting. |

 Q3 *"Attractiveness is not about size."*

a) Make a list of all the things that you think make someone fanciable: stuff like "is not an axe-murderer", "clean fingernails", "no mullet", "green eyes".

b) Put your list in order with the most important at the top and the most irrelevant at the bottom. Where does "size" come?

 Q4 Gary has bad breath and only one topic of conversation — Gary. He's miserable because he thinks he's overweight, and he thinks that makes him unpopular.

Write an action plan for Gary, telling him how to find out if he really is overweight, and how to lose weight if he needs to.

What advice can you give Gary about making himself a bit more popular?

Section Five — Food

Eating Healthy Stuff

Q1 Match up each type of food with the reason it's good for you:

| bread, rice, pasta, etc. | fatty foods | sugary foods | fruit and vegetables | fish, meat, beans, nuts |

Give you energy. Calcium in dairy foods keeps teeth and bones strong.

Full of protein which helps your body grow and repair itself.

Give you energy. Taste good and make you happy.

Give you energy. Energy from these foods keeps you going longest.

Packed with vitamins and fibre to keep everything running smoothly.

Q2 Roughly how much of what you eat should be...

a) fish and meat (or other high-protein food)

b) dairy products

c) starchy food

d) sweet sugary food

e) fruit and vegetables

Choose your answers from this box — you'll need some of them more than once.

$\frac{1}{3}$ $\frac{1}{6}$ $\frac{1}{12}$

Q3 What types of food should each of these people cut back on, or eat more of?

a) **DICK**

Monday
Bacon, sausage, bread
Pie and chips
Deep pan pizza
Tuesday
Bacon sandwich
Fish and chips
Special fried rice

b) **DAMIAN**

Monday
Toast
Chocolate
Lasagne and salad
Chocolate; ice-cream
Soup and bread
Tuesday
Toast
Chocolate
Chilli con carne, salad and chips
Cake; ice-cream
Tuna salad

c) **DAVE**

Monday
Cornflakes
Toast
Rice and veggie curry
Tuesday
Cornflakes
Egg sandwich
Baked potato and beans

DISCUSSION QUESTION **Q4** Write down everything you ate yesterday.

Do you think you ate a reasonably healthy, balanced diet yesterday?

Compare what you ate with what other people in your group ate.
Write an action plan for each person in the group with suggestions for healthier eating.

Section Five — Food

Learning to Cook

Q1 Copy the paragraph about prepackaged food and fill in the gaps using the words on the right:

> Home-cooked food is .... than prepackaged food. It has far more .... and .... because it's fresher.
>
> To make prepackaged food last longer, manufacturers put in .... They also add extra ...., ... and .... to cover up the fact that the food tastes bland.
>
> Prepackaged food also works out more .... than home-made food.

Words: fat, minerals, expensive, sugar, vitamins, chemical additives, salt, healthier

Q2 Salmonella Sue's kitchen is foul. Say what needs sorting out for a) to d) below.

a) The cream's stored in a nice warm cupboard near the boiler.

b) After handling raw meat, Sue always wipes her hands on a tea towel, then uses the tea towel to polish all the fruit in the fruit bowl.

c) After she's been to the loo, Salmonella Sue never washes her hands. She gets right on with baking some lovely cakes for the grandchildren.

d) When there's a little spill, Sue doesn't wipe it up. She waits for one of the cats to lick it away.

Q3 This is what Bob thinks about cooking. Write a few sentences suggesting a different point of view.

> "Cooking's really hard and I don't have time — it must take ages to make anything nice. Anyway, isn't cooking my mum's job? I mean, what else has she got to do when she gets in from work? And when I leave home I can heat stuff up from the freezer. It'll be great."

Q4 Write down these headings: "Good for Me", "I Really Like It" and "Quick / Easy".

Write the names of foods you've eaten in the last few days under the different headings. It's fine if some things go under two or three headings.

Have a look at the lists other people in your group made. Do people mostly eat what they like, what's good for them, or what's convenient?

Enjoy your meal...

There's a lot of snobby rubbish talked about food. I mean, if you really care whether your sun-dried tomatoes are French or Italian, then good for you. The rest of us will get on with learning to make an omelette.

Section Five — Food

Respecting People

Q1 Match up each definition with the right word from the box:

> disrespect   respect

a) Treat people however you like, without thinking about their thoughts or feelings.

b) Treat people as you'd want to be treated, and think about their thoughts and feelings.

Q2 Annoying Anton has been constantly picking on people in his class. Sometimes it gets fairly serious. Which of these is Anton likely to get?

- In trouble with the police.
- A free holiday in the Seychelles.
- Lots of friends.
- A load of grief at school.
- A load of grief at home.

Q3 Explain what's wrong with each of these:

a) *Teasing someone for having cheap-looking clothes isn't serious, just a bit of a laugh.*

b) *Unpopular people like being teased — it's attention after all.*

c) *I can take a bit of teasing, so surely it's OK if I tease other people.*

d) *Old people's brains are slowing down. They can't really tell what you're saying to them, so you can say whatever you like.*

DISCUSSION QUESTION

Q4 Which of these sentences do you think is right?

"Everyone deserves equal respect."

"You should only give respect to people who deserve it."

If you don't think either sentence is quite right, write your own, saying what you think.

Dealing with People

Q1 Which of these are ways people bully others?

> taking money off people   being insulting   shoving people around   stealing things from people
>
> telling someone the way to the bus stop   picking on someone for the way they look   eating a hamburger
>
> beating someone up   making someone the butt of all your jokes   having a row

Q2 What's the difference between bullying for homophobic or racist reasons and other types of bullying?

Q3 Answer these questions about peer pressure:

a) Explain what "peer pressure" is.

b) Write a list of at least five things people sometimes do because of peer pressure.

Do what I say, or I'll knock yer block off.

Q4 Choose the right set of words to finish off each sentence:

a) People who **stand up for themselves / always give in to other people** get more respect.

b) You **can / can't** stand up for yourself without walking all over other people.

DISCUSSION QUESTION Q5 Write a script for the situation described below. It can be really short — just a few lines is fine.

Ian's talking to Marta. He accidentally says something that really offends her. Ian refuses to apologise. Ian and Marta have a blazing row.

Next, write as many different endings as you can for your script with Ian apologising for what he's said or done or smoothing the situation over.

DISCUSSION QUESTION Q6 You've noticed some girls in Year 7 giving another girl a really hard time.

Write down what you could say to them to persuade them to stop — without being a bully yourself.

Section Six — Looking After Yourself

Dealing with Trouble

Q1 Find the right ending for each sentence below, from the box on the right.

a) Try to avoid...

b) Don't react aggressively if people hassle you...

c) Tell somebody what's going on...

d) If the people hassling you are doing it because they're prejudiced against you...

> ...as it could make things worse.
>
> ...even if you feel awkward or embarrassed about it.
>
> ...you should think about getting the police involved.
>
> ...confrontations.

Q2 What's the web address for "Bullying Online"?

Q3 Look at each pair below. Say which is the more sensible thing to do to avoid bullying and explain why.

a)
- Spending your lunch break sitting on your own, down at the end of the sports field.
- Spending your lunch break with other people or where lots of other people are around.

b)
- Always going home by the same route.
- Varying your route home.

c)
- Making plenty of friends, or at least being on chatting terms with as many people as possible.
- Being fairly antisocial. Keeping yourself to yourself.

d)
- Telling a teacher or another adult about bullying as soon as possible.
- Ignoring the bullying — they'll get bored and move on to someone else eventually.

Q4 Choose the right set of words to finish off each sentence:

a) Threatening emails and text messages are **legal / illegal**.

b) If you decide to tell an adult about being bullied and they don't seem to take it all that seriously, **give up / try telling someone else**.

c) Reacting to violence with violence **will just lead to more violence / should sort things out**.

DISCUSSION QUESTION Q5 A lot of people think Steve's gay. A few people in his year have been giving him physical and verbal abuse for it.

Write down a list of things Steve can do to deal with the bullying.

Section Six — Looking After Yourself

Surviving Home Life

Q1 True or false?

   a) Most families have blazing rows every now and then.

   b) Most families find communication very easy and straightforward.

Q2 Kirk's a really poor communicator. It makes all sorts of situations at home much worse than they need to be. Explain how he could have handled each of these situations better:

   a) Kirk's sister Kerry is crying and trying to tell him something. He says, "Not now, I'm watching *Big Brother*," and turns up the sound on the telly.

   b) The other day one of Kirk's mates took him out for a driving lesson in Kirk's mum's car. He didn't ask if he could take the car, in case his mum said no.

   c) On his driving lesson Kirk reverses into a bollard in a car park. When he gets home he parks the car and doesn't say anything. When his mum blames his sister he still doesn't say anything.

   d) Kirk's mum asks him straight out whether he's got anything to do with the dented bumper. There was a burger box in the back of the car and Kirk's a burger fiend. Kirk says, "It's nothing to do with me. Why don't you ask Kerry — she's the fat one round here."

   e) Kerry gets really upset and tearful. Kirk's mum says he's got to apologise. He says, "Whatever," and goes out for the rest of the day.

 Q3 Imagine you've got to break some really big news to your family.

   It can be anything you like — you're gay, you're pregnant, you robbed the Co-op, you poisoned the cat, etc.

   Write a script where you break the news gently and their reactions are as good as you can expect. Then write another one where you break the news badly and get the worst possible reactions.

 Q4 Make a list of problems and situations that create stress in families.

   Base the list on your own experiences and what you've heard about others/seen on the telly.

You can choose your friends, but you can't choose your family...

"Sometimes even folks from the happiest families feel like screaming with claustrophobia, smashing plates and slamming the door behind them for good." From *G'Night Y'All*, the autobiography of John-Boy Walton, 1977.

Section Six — Looking After Yourself

Keeping Safe

Q1 Explain to each person why what they're saying isn't really common sense:

a) **Naive Nelly**
"Everyone I've ever met was really great. Everyone I know now is really great. So I reckon everyone I'm going to meet from now on is going to be really great."

b) **Paranoid Pete**
"You never know when the next psycho or rapist or escaped serial murderer is going to come round the corner. That's why I stay at home with my budgies."

Q2 What's the better option in each pair below? Explain why.

a) Walking home the long way along the main roads with streetlighting.
Cutting through the alleys and down by the canal.

b) It's pouring with rain and a stranger pulls over and offers you a lift. You take it.
It's pouring with rain and a stranger pulls over and offers you a lift. You don't take it.

c) Sarah's in a club with her mates. Sarah thinks she sees a man drop something in her mate Lisa's glass while she's dancing, so she goes and pours it away. Lisa's really annoyed.
Sarah's in a club with her mates. She thinks she sees someone drop something in her mate Lisa's glass. She thinks, "That's a bit funny."

d) Lisa gets chatting to some blokes. She's a bit tipsy. They ask her back to their flat. She goes.
Lisa gets chatting to some blokes. She's a bit tipsy. They ask her back to their flat. She asks for their phone number and says she'll come round in the week.

Q3 You're a bloke walking home at night on your own. You see a woman alone ahead of you on the pavement. Should you:

a) Speed up and overtake her?

b) Just keep walking at the same distance from her?

c) Cross to the other side of the road?

Q4 If you're being attacked are you more likely to get help if you shout "Rape!" or "Fire!"?

DISCUSSION QUESTION Q5 Write a list of DOs and DON'Ts for people using chat rooms.

Section Six — Looking After Yourself

Abuse

Q1 Copy the paragraph and fill in the gaps using the best words below. You won't need all the words.

anyone *power or authority* *young children* *ask for help*

violent *know the victim well* *sexual* *are strangers* *threaten*

> An abuser takes advantage of their .... over somebody else to do something to the victim which the victim does not want.
> The abuse can be .... or ....
> It's possible for .... to become a victim of abuse — so everybody needs to be aware of the dangers.
> Most abuse is carried out by people who .... Abusers often .... even worse harm if the victim tells anyone what's going on. This can make it really hard for victims of abuse to ....

Q2 Which of these boxes could be describing a case of abuse?

> A boy isn't allowed to go on the school trip because his mum can't afford it.

> An eleven year-old boy is at home on his own at least five nights a week. There's no food in the house and he doesn't have any money.

> As a punishment for breaking a cup a woman won't give her daughter pocket money for two weeks.

> A girl's dad thrashes her for staying out late and she ends up with a broken wrist.

Q3 How would you contact...

a) the NSPCC? Give the phone number and email address.

b) Childline? Give the phone number.

Q4 What signs might there be that somebody you know is being abused?

DISCUSSION QUESTION Q5 You strongly suspect that someone in your class has got problems at home, and they may be being abused in some way.

Work out how you're going to deal with the situation.

Section Six — Looking After Yourself

Running Away

Q1 Write down as many reasons as you can why somebody might run away from home.

Q2 True or false?

   a) You can legally leave home at 16.

   b) If somebody runs away from home and they're under 16, the police will be involved in searching for them.

   c) If you explain why you want to leave home to the housing department at the council, they'll probably find you a place of your own in a few days or so.

   d) If you sleep rough in winter, it can get cold enough to kill you.

   e) You're at risk of robbery and rape when you sleep rough.

   f) Most hostels have lots of spare beds, especially in London, so you won't actually have to sleep on the streets if you don't fancy it.

There was a rumour about a spare hostel bed.

   g) A lot of rough sleepers end up as alcoholics because they can't face their lives if they think about them sober.

Q3 What's the phone number for the Shelter helpline?

 Q4 These are all places you could end up if you run away from home:

- on the street
- in a hostel
- on a mate's floor
- in a social services care home
- back at home
- in a squat

Which ones do you think are reasonable temporary places to stay?
Which ones do you think are reasonable permanent places to stay?

Q5 Shanya really wants to leave home. She's 15 and still at school and she's going to go on and do AS and A-levels.

What are her options?

Decide on the best option for Shanya.

Running away can get you in a load more trouble...
Think very very hard before you leave home with nowhere to go. If you decide you really have to get out for your own safety, or because you're just too miserable to stay, find somewhere to go <u>before</u> you leave.

Section Six — Looking After Yourself

Section Seven — Mental Health

Coping with Change

Q1 Which of these feelings are people likely to have when something seriously bad happens to them?

| guilt | feeling numb | anger | sadness | despair |

Q2 When you're really upset, which of the things below will make you feel better and which will make you feel worse? Write "better" or "worse" for each one.

a) Sitting on your own listening to depressing CDs.

b) Talking to other people who are upset about the same thing.

c) Eating ice-cream.

d) Giving people the brush-off if they try and talk to you about how you feel.

e) Pretending everything's fine.

This is likely to be different for everyone.

Q3 When Phil's grandma died, he went through all sorts of different feelings. Read through them and then put them in a sensible order:

There's no right answer to this one, by the way.

Went bowling with his mates and had a really good time. When he got home he realised he hadn't thought about his Gran at all and felt guilty and upset.

Didn't want to talk to anyone about it.

Started crying and couldn't stop for ages.

Felt really angry at his Gran for dying. Felt like she'd done it on purpose, even though he knew that didn't make sense.

Started thinking more about good things his Gran did when she was alive, and less about the fact that she was dead.

 Q4 Your cousin lives in New York, and his parents are getting divorced. Write him a friendly letter or email offering him some advice.

 Q5 Think about a few of the most serious things that have happened to you.

This one's not meant to make you feel miserable. If it does, make a list of good stuff that's happened to you.

Try and remember how long it took to feel better.

What kind of things helped you feel better? How do you feel about the events now?

Feeling Down

Q1 Which of these are symptoms of depression?

Tired all the time	Finding it hard to concentrate	Sneezing	Forgetful
Panic attacks	Out-of-date mobile phone	No energy	Major mood swings
Hairy palms	Waking up feeling exhausted	Stiff joints	Crying really easily

Q2 Copy and complete the paragraph, choosing the right words from below to fill in the gaps (you may need to use the same word twice):

symptoms   most of the time   lots of   mind   most weird

doctor   a couple of weeks   twenty-four hours   every now and then   glands

> Depression isn't just "feeling down". It's an illness that affects the .... People who have depression feel bad about themselves and their lives .... people have it at some point in their lives.
>
> There are lots of different .... of depression. If you're depressed you don't always get them all at the same time. If you do have some of the .... and they don't go away after ...., you need to go to the ....

Q3 "I've lost my earrings," squealed Cornelia Compton-Corset. "I'm so totally depressed."

a) Would you say Cornelia is genuinely depressed?
b) Explain your answer to a).

Q4 What can you do from day to day to avoid getting too down?

DISCUSSION QUESTION Q5 Gina is feeling really low — all the time. She thinks she's got full-blown depression.

What should Gina do?

Make a list of questions to help Gina work out whether she's really depressed, and suggest what she can do if she is.

If you're depressed get help — don't let things get worse...

Lots of people do get depressed at some point — but that doesn't mean you <u>definitely</u> will or that if you do you'll never feel better. Getting help is really important — it helps you feel just a bit better straight away.

Section Seven — Mental Health

Stress, Anxiety and Panic Attacks

Q1 Stress isn't an illness, but it can make you ill. Which of the following health problems can be caused by stress? Choose the right words from each pair.

a) low blood pressure / high blood pressure

b) higher risk of heart attacks and strokes / higher risk of incontinence

c) headaches / earaches

d) hungry all the time / can't get to sleep

e) constipation / corns

Gerry's stressed.
It's easy to read the signs.
But then Gerry's a cartoon.

Q2 Stressed Barry is always stressed. Write down all the sentences that describe a stressed person:

When Barry misses a train he says "Oh, good. Now I can sit on a bench in the sunshine and read the paper."

Barry swears under his breath at people who walk slower than him in shops.

When Bernie offers to help Barry out, Barry shouts at Bernie and tells him to "go away".

Barry leaves work early and goes for a walk in the park.

Barry spills a cup of coffee and blows his top.

Barry stays at work till midnight because he doesn't think he'll have time to do everything tomorrow.

Barry does ten things at a time and doesn't do any of them properly.

Q3 Below are the things you should do if somebody has a panic attack. Put them in the right order.

- If they don't seem much better, get them to do another ten slow breaths into the bag.
- Open the bag up and give it to the person having the panic attack.
- Find a paper bag — quick as you can.
- Tell them to put the bag down and breathe normally for a bit.
- Tell them to breathe in and out slowly with the bag over their mouth and nose. They should breathe into the bag at least ten times — or more if their breathing's very shaky.

Q4 *Everyone feels a bit anxious at times, but for some people it's a long-term problem.*

a) Write down the symptoms of anxiety.

b) What can your doctor do if anxiety is a serious problem for you?

Q5 *[DISCUSSION QUESTION]* *AAAARGH! Exams are coming. I've done no revision. I've got too much to do. ****!*

This person seems a bit stressed. Write an action plan for them explaining how they can avoid getting totally stressed out.

Section Seven — Mental Health

Suicide and Self-Harm

Q1 Copy and complete the paragraph, using words from below:

the only way   far fewer   more   even fewer   normal   many

> .... people have suicidal feelings at some point in their lives. .... people act on their feelings and make definite plans to kill themselves. .... actually commit suicide. Feeling unhappy is a .... part of life, but suicide is never .... to escape your unhappiness. People who commit suicide leave .... unhappiness behind them for their friends and family.

Q2 Choose the best set of words to finish off each sentence:

a) Attempted suicide **needs to be taken very seriously / is not that serious**.

b) People who attempt suicide **do not want help or support / need help and support**.

c) Some people attempt suicide as a way of **showing they're unhappy / making you feel guilty**.

d) Some people attempt suicide but **don't really mean it / hope they'll be found before they die**.

Q3 Answer these questions about self-harm:

a) Is there one simple reason why people harm themselves?

b) What are the most common ways that people harm themselves?

c) If you recognise that you have a problem with self-harm, what should you do?

d) If someone you know is harming themselves, what's the best way of helping them?

e) Are the injuries people give themselves ever serious enough to need medical treatment?

Q4 There are lots of different people and organisations who will help people who have suicidal feelings, or feelings that lead them to harm themselves.

How many can you think of off the top of your head? Make a list.

Find out full contact details for each person or organisation on your list.

Eating Disorders

Q1 Write 'True' or 'False' for each of these statements:

a) People with anorexia and bulimia believe they are overweight, even though they're often dangerously underweight.

b) The best way to tackle anorexia is just to sit down with the person and make them eat a big tasty meal.

c) Anorexia and bulimia are digestive problems.

d) Problems with anorexia and bulimia often start when people are depressed or worried.

Q2 Which of these can be caused by anorexia?

flaky toenails   periods stop   dry hair   dry skin   hairy skin

always cold   sex hormone levels drop   red, painful rash   constant sneezing

Q3 Bulimia is a vicious circle. Put these stages of the cycle in order:

| Uses laxatives or vomiting to get rid of binge food. | "Binges" — overeats. | Feels guilty about overeating. |

| Gets desperate for food. | Goes back to strict dieting. | Diets very strictly. Possibly doesn't eat at all. |

Q4 Which of these are side-effects of bulimia?

sore throat   rapid hair growth   zinc deficiency

cramp   tooth decay   damage to vocal chords

 Q5 Kerry thinks her friend May is bulimic and needs help.

Decide on the best advice to give Kerry for how to help May.

Section Seven — Mental Health

Dealing with Mental Health

Q1 If you're feeling low, how long should you wait before seeing your doctor about a mental health problem?

Q2 What can each of these organisations help with?

   a) ANRED

   b) SANE

   c) MIND

Q3 From each pair, choose the best advice for helping a friend with a mental health problem:

   a) • If your friend says they need to talk, don't let them go on and on about how they feel. Wallowing in self-pity never did anyone any good.
      • If your friend needs to talk, let them talk. Listen to what they've got to say.

   b) • You can't make people tell you their problems. The best thing to do is just make it clear you're ready to listen and give your support if that's what your friend wants.
      • What your friend really needs is to get everything off their chest. Keep asking them what's wrong till they tell you. It doesn't matter if you annoy them or upset them.

   c) • Call a taxi and bundle your friend down to the GP's surgery as soon as possible.
      • Even if you don't think they'll want to talk to you, you could always suggest other people for them to talk to, like their doctor or the Samaritans.

   d) • If your friend gets stroppy or difficult, then don't bother with them any more. They're just not worth the effort.
      • Don't give up on your friend, even if the illness makes them difficult to get on with. Your support will be helping them get better, even if they don't seem all that appreciative now.

Q4 Do you know anyone who's had mental health problems?

   You don't need to say who they are if you don't want to, but you could talk about:

   • how it changed the way they behaved

   • whether it changed your relationship with them

   • whether you were able to help

   • whether they got better and how

It's all about knowing when you need help...

You can't go round all day worrying about getting depressed or anorexic. But it is a good idea to know what the most common problems are and where to get help, so if something does go wrong you can sort it out.

Section Eight — Drugs

Why People Take Drugs

Q1 Write out this paragraph and fill in the gaps using the words below:

body chemistry   enjoy   side-effects   mind   body

> Drugs change your .... This makes your ...., ... or both feel different. Some people start taking drugs because they .... these effects. Unfortunately, not all the effects of drugs are enjoyable and some have serious ....

Q2 Write down all the sentences that describe the side-effects of drugs:

The side-effects of drugs only damage your physical health.

Some side-effects, like hangovers, hit you in the short-term.

The side-effects of drugs can damage your mental and physical health.

Side-effects are never serious and clear up by themselves.

Some side-effects, like lung cancer, are lethal.

Some side-effects hit you after several years.

Q3 True or false?

a) If you get a police record for possessing or supplying drugs you may be refused entry to the United States for life.

b) You only get a criminal record for possession or dealing if you're convicted in a court of law.

c) A criminal record lasts forever.

d) A criminal record can affect your chances of getting a job.

Q4 These are some of the reasons why people take recreational drugs:

| Curiosity | Escapism | Enjoyment | Image | Boredom | Rebellion |

Which of these reasons for taking drugs make sense to you? Which don't?

Are there any other reasons for taking drugs that you can think of? Do these make sense?

Section Eight — Drugs

Nicotine

Q1 What are the physical effects of nicotine? Choose the right words from each pair:

a) Inhaling cigarette smoke **raises / lowers** the smoker's heart rate.

b) Inhaling cigarette smoke **raises / lowers** the smoker's blood pressure.

c) Smoking gives the smoker a feeling of **relaxation / excitement**.

Q2 Explain what makes smoking:

a) physically addictive

b) mentally addictive

Q3 Which of these can be caused by smoking?

lung cancer   *emphysema*   *bronchitis*   *stroke*

mouth cancer   *heart disease*   *lip cancer*

cancer of the throat   *peripheral vascular disease in the legs, leading to amputation*   *coronary artery disease*

Phil was never at his best before the first cigarette of the day.

Q4 How does smoking affect the smoker's...

a) skin?

b) teeth?

c) gums?

d) breath?

Q5 *It's pretty weird how so many people smoke when it's so obviously unhealthy.*

In your experience, why do people start smoking?

Why do people carry on smoking?

Q6 *Kirsty's been smoking for five years and wants to stop. She's finding it really hard.*

Come up with a list of reasons why she should stop.

Write down all the ways of giving up smoking that you've heard of.

Section Eight — Drugs

Alcohol

Q1   True or false?

   a) Alcohol can raise your mood, but it can also bring you down.

   b) If you get caught drinking in a pub and you're underage, the landlord gets fined, but you'll just get a ticking off.

   c) Alcohol makes you more coordinated and speeds up your reaction times.

   d) Drinks take five to ten minutes to have a big effect. If you've had a lot of drinks in a row very quickly, you'll keep getting more and more drunk for some time after your last drink.

   e) A couple of units of alcohol a night is a major health risk.

Q2   Copy out this table and fill in the gaps:

Type of drink	Usual % of alcohol
Spirits	
	10-15%
	3-7%
Alcopops	
	no alcohol

Q3   "Hic. This wedding's been going on for hours. I've drunk a bit more champagne than I planned. I feel way too drunk and I'm going to have a stinking hangover tomorrow."

Write some tips for the person above on what they should do about being more drunk than planned, and about tomorrow's hangover. Mention coffee, soft drinks, water and paracetamol.

Q4   Explain to each drinker why the way she drinks is a bad idea:

   a) *TRACEY*
   Doesn't drink at all during the week. On Friday nights drinks vodka and lemonade from 7.00pm to 2.00am.

   b) *RACHEL*
   Opens a bottle of wine with dinner every night. Usually finishes it.

Q5   Heavy drinking, whether it's binge drinking or every day, can have serious effects on your life.

Make a list of the effects heavy drinking can have on your health, your wallet, and your social life.

Section Eight — Drugs

Cannabis

Q1 Which of these can be caused by cannabis?

> giggliness • weight loss • nausea • paranoia • thought process gets sharper • cravings for junk food • aggressive behaviour • improved sexual performance • sleepiness • spaced-out feeling

Q2 Copy and complete the paragraph using the words below. You won't need all of them.

mental   in the past   colour   plastic   how they're feeling   type

how hungry they are   in one day   more   evidence

> How cannabis affects people who use it depends on the .... they're using and .... when they take it. People who've smoked a lot of cannabis .... will need to smoke .... to get the same effect. Cannabis has most of the same health risks as tobacco, and there is also .... to suggest that cannabis use can be linked to certain .... health problems, such as schizophrenia and depression.

Q3 Is it illegal to...

a) smoke cannabis?

b) be in a room with people smoking cannabis?

c) have cannabis in your pocket?

d) buy or sell cannabis?

DISCUSSION QUESTION Q4 "Smoking cannabis is the first step down the rocky road to a life of crime and addiction." Do you agree?

DISCUSSION QUESTION Q5 Smoking cannabis, drinking alcohol and smoking cigarettes are all bad for your health.

Why do you think cannabis is illegal and alcohol and smoking are legal?

Cannabis — the drug of peace, love and 2-10 for dealing...
Cannabis is less dangerous and addictive than, say, heroin or crack. But it can make you behave like a right idiot — or worse, lose all your common sense and end up in awkward or tricky situations. So look out.

Section Eight — Drugs

Ecstasy

Q1 Which of these is another name for ecstasy?

   MAMA   MDMA   ADAM   DAMM

Q2 Ecstasy itself isn't lethal. Why have people died after taking E?

Q3 Draw a table like the one below and then fill it in with as much information as you can about ecstasy.

pleasant effects	unpleasant effects	physical effects

Q4 Which of these statements is correct?

a) As the ecstasy wears off you feel more and more relaxed.

b) As the ecstasy wears off you feel cold, tired and emotionally very shaky.

c) The feeling the day after you've taken ecstasy is just like a hangover.

Q5 True or false?

a) Some dealers sell aspirin and pretend it's ecstasy.

b) Some dealers sell pills which are a mixture of ecstasy and other drugs and pretend they're pure ecstasy.

c) If you buy from a dealer you know, you can be sure you're getting pure ecstasy.

Q6 Ecstasy could have serious long-term effects.

a) What might those long-term effects be?

b) Why isn't anyone sure what the long-term effects of ecstasy are?

Q7 *"If people kill themselves by taking drugs it's their own silly fault."*

Do you agree? If it's not the drug-taker's fault, whose fault is it?

Section Eight — Drugs

Acid, Mushrooms and Speed

Q1 Copy these sentences, filling in the gaps with one of the words from the box:

a) .... affect the body.

b) .... affect the mind.

> stimulants
>
> psychedelic drugs

Q2 How is acid usually taken...

a) as a pill?

b) injected?

c) on a square of paper?

d) smoked?

Dave believed everything his friends told him about drugs — even the stuff about it being cool to smoke magic mushrooms.

Q3 Put these stages of an acid "trip" into order:

| As the acid wears off the user experiences a 'comedown' and can feel very uneasy and emotionally fragile. | Over the next few hours the user sees strange visual effects, including hallucinations — things that aren't really there. |

| During the 'head trip' time seems to stand still. This is the most intense phase of the trip. | About half an hour after taking the tab the user sees trails behind moving objects and other weird effects. |

Q4 Why should people who have mental health problems definitely steer clear of acid?

Q5 Choose the right set of words from each pair to finish off these sentences:

a) Speed is also known as **amphetamine / MDMA**.

b) Speed is taken by **smoking or injection / snorting or injection**.

c) Speed suppresses your **appetite / instincts**.

d) Speed gives the user lots of **short-term / long-term** energy.

e) When the speed wears off, the user feels **refreshed / exhausted**.

DISCUSSION QUESTION Q6 In the 1960s a lot of musicians claimed that they got creative inspiration from taking acid.

Why do you think they said this?

Do you think this is a good enough reason for taking acid?

Section Eight — Drugs

Heroin, Cocaine and Crack

Q1 Copy and complete the paragraph using the words below. You don't need all the words.

> one hit   high   every day   two hits
> two or three times a year   mugging and robbing   addiction

> For some people, ... of heroin is enough to lead them to ....
> They enjoy the blissed-out .... and become desperate for another one.
> Once somebody is addicted, they crave a hit .... If it's difficult for them to find the
> money to pay for the next hit, they may end up .... people to raise the cash.

Q2 Describe how a heroin addict may end up feeling at each of these stages of giving up:

a) After 8-24 hours.

b) After 7-10 days.

c) During the months following the last hit.

Q3 Choose the right set of words from each pair to finish off these sentences:

a) Taking coke tends to make people **self-centred and arrogant / relaxed and easy-going**.

b) Coke is **one of the cheapest drugs / one of the most expensive drugs**.

c) A coke high is **very long / very short**.

d) Crack is **much more / much less** addictive than cocaine.

e) A crack comedown is **OK / absolutely horrific**.

f) Taking **a large dose or several hits of / just a small amount of** coke or crack can lead to anxiety, paranoia and sometimes hallucinations.

Q4 Write three headings — "Heroin", "Cocaine" and "Crack" — and put each of the following points under the right heading. You can put them under more than one heading if you need to.

> crystals   injected   risk of addiction
> risk of nose cartilage collapsing
> made from the opium poppy   risk of HIV or other diseases carried in the blood
> smoked   overdose can be fatal   white powder   snorted

Q5 Cocaine has got a reputation as a relatively glamorous drug.

Why do you think this is?

Do you think cocaine deserves its image?

Section Eight — Drugs

Solvents and Other Nasty Narcotics

Q1 Write two headings — "DXM" and "Solvents" — and sort out the information below so that each point is under the right heading.

- can cause death by heart failure or suffocation (if taken through the mouth)
- full name is dextromethorphan
- can make the user vomit and/or pass out
- can cause mental health problems
- taken by inhalation
- a psychedelic drug
- found in cough medicines

Q2 Copy and complete the paragraph by choosing the right words from below:

for you   tranquillisers   make you feel poorly   by a qualified doctor
be lethal   antibiotics   prescription drugs   addictive

.... are drugs which are usually used for curing illness. Taking drugs which weren't prescribed .... is very dangerous. It's all too easy to take too much and the wrong dose can .... Some prescription drugs, especially .... , are just as .... as other kinds of drug.

Q3 Say what drug's being described in each box:

- A horse anaesthetic.
- Used by bodybuilders for muscle development and by clubbers to lower inhibitions.
- Has been used for "date rape".
- A prescription tranquilliser.

Q4 Why is it dangerous to take combinations of drugs?

 Q5 "Drugs will ruin your life."

Do you think this is a reasonable statement?

Work out a sentence or two that sum up your attitude to drugs (all the ones you know about, not just the ones on this page) and compare it with others in your group.

These things are the lowest of the low — steer well clear...

If you're honest with yourself about the consequences, ALL drugs are pretty grim. If you ever end up being offered/tempted to take stuff, don't just take it on a whim or cos you're bored — it's more serious than that.

Section Eight — Drugs